A Handbook for Church Treasurers

Concise Information for a Complicated Task

By Edd Breeden

(Intentionally Blank)

A Handbook for Church Treasurers

By

Edd Breeden

Online, www.breeden.us

Email edd@breeden.us

Copyright @2019 by Edd Breeden.

All Rights Reserved.

In accordance with the U.S. Copyright Act of 1976, the scanning, uploading, and electronic sharing of any part of this book without the permission of the author/publisher constitutes unlawful piracy and theft of the author's intellectual property. If you would like to use material from the book (other than for review purposes), prior written permission must be obtained by contacting the author at edd@breeden.us. Thank you for our support of the author's rights.

ISBN 9781794387355

Scripture quotations taken from the New American Standard Bible®,
Copyright © 1960, 1962, 1963, 1968, 1971, 1972, 1973,
1975, 1977, 1995 by The Lockman Foundation
Used by permission." (www.Lockman.org)
"Scripture quotations taken from the NASB."

For all of the hearty volunteers
who faithfully watch over
the finances of the church.

Thank you for your service.

OTHER BOOKS BY EDD BREEDEN

Available in paperback and digital format.

- **Autobiographical**
- The Drunken Preacher, My Life as a Servant of Jesus

- **Christian Living Titles.**
- Discipleship Training Manual.
- Generous Living, Jesus Teaches about Wealth.
  - Vol. 1, Matthew.
  - Vol. 2, Matthew.
- Prayer, A Practical Guide to Spending Time with God.
- Unmasked and Loved, A Resource for Peer-Counselors, Co-Authored with the late Zelpha Blythe-Persson.

- **Commentaries.**
- 40 Mornings with the Apostle John,
  - A Study of the Revelations 1-3.
- Ephesians Amplified.
- Galatians Amplified.
- Philippians Amplified.
- Coming Soon, Colossians Amplified.

- **Study Guides, Bible Studies.**
- Advent Study Guides.

- **Pastor Helps.**
- Christmas Eve Candlelight Service.
- Christmas Sermons.
- Christmas Sermons Vol. 2.
- Worship Services for Special Occasions, Baker House Publishers, out of print but often available online.

- **Church Helps.**
- The Church Treasurers Manual.
- The Handbook for Church Treasurers.

ABOUT THE AUTHOR, EDD BREEDEN

Edd received his Masters of Divinity degree from Fuller Theological Seminary, Pasadena, CA. in 1974 and has pastored Presbyterian Churches in Minnesota and California since that time. His emphasis in seminary centered on Biblical languages and Bible Study and has continued through the years to seek a deeper understanding of the Scriptures. At times teaching four to five studies each week, Edd has a solid grasp of the teachings found in the Scriptures and an ability to clearly unpack the meanings and applications for those who listen.

He recently retired from day-to-day pastoring and lives in Scotts Valley, CA, with his wife. Married in 1968, they have four children and 9 living grandchildren in the area and love spending time with family and friends.

Edd grew up as an Air Force Brat; living in Ohio, Louisiana, Puerto Rico, and California. He attended Santa Barbara City College and later graduated from the University of California at Santa Barbara in 1970 with a Bachelor's degree in Mathematics.

Edd is the author of an autobiography called, The Drunken Preacher, and a variety of books available online; including Biblical Commentaries on a number of Bible Books, Study Guides, Topics of interest to Christians and Resources for Pastors.

He loves to write, teach, read, play golf, and listen to Country Western Music.

(Intentionally Blank)

This Handbook was originally produced for

Church Treasurers

in the Presbytery of San Jose

a member of the Presbyterian Church (U.S.A.) and for church Treasurers throughout our denomination.

Others should feel free to use the manual knowing that much of the terminology pertains most directly to churches within the PCUSA.

The word "Session" refers to the Board of Elders. In many organizations it is just the Board of Directors.

This Handbook is a concise form of a larger Manual; The Church Treasurer's Manual. This Handbook is meant as an easy guide to the regular tasks of church finances. If you require more information on some subjects the Manual is available for download and contains easy navigation.

(Intentionally Blank)

This Handbook is intended as a reference guide to help you when you have questions. It is recommended that all church Treasurers keep up to date on changes in the laws and policies of your state as they do change from time to time and also vary from state to state.

*If at any time you find an error in spelling, grammar, content, or if you have thoughts on something that should be included in this Handbook, you have another way to do something and want to share it with others, etc. please email **edd@breeden.us** with what you have found so that we can keep the Handbook as accurate, complete and helpful as possible.*

Important Disclaimer

While this Handbook is provided in the hope it will assist you generally in answering questions, **this document does not attempt to render legal, accounting, or other professional advice or services** to you. Please consult a competent professional attorney or tax advisor, where you live, who is familiar with local non-profit laws and policies.

(Intentionally Blank)

Contents of the Book

General Responsibilities

Intro: Functions of a Church Treasurer.　　Pg. 17

1. Introduction to Church Finances.　　Pg. 21
2. The make-up of a Financial Team.　　Pg. 22
3. A system of Record Keeping.　　Pg. 23
4. Defining your Financial Policies.　　Pg. 26
5. Accurate and beneficial Bookkeeping.　　Pg. 28
6. Simple and clear Documentation.　　Pg. 29
7. Reconciling the bank accounts.　　Pg. 30
8. Conflict of Interest concerns.　　Pg. 31
9. Passwords and Keys; Office Security.　　Pg. 32
10. How long should you Retain Records?　　Pg. 33
11. The required Annual Review or Audit.　　Pg. 36
12. The Annual Review Checklist.　　Pg. 37

Revenues

13. Understanding Revenues. (Income).　　Pg. 39
14. Developing a Gift Acceptance Policy.　　Pg. 40
15. Memorial Giving and Special Gifts.　　Pg. 42
16. Procedures for Counting Offerings.　　Pg. 43
17. Maintaining member's Giving Records.　　Pg. 44
18. Data Management.　　Pg. 45
19. Sending Contributions Receipts.　　Pg. 46
20. Church Enterprises; Book Stores.　　Pg. 47
21. Reporting Unrelated Business Income.　　Pg. 48
22. Thoughts on Stewardship.　　Pg. 49

23. Planning for Investments.   Pg. 50
24. Having an Investment Policy.   Pg. 51

Disbursements

25. Understanding Disbursements.   Pg. 55
26. Keeping track of Vendors.   Pg. 56
27. Checkbooks and Authorized Signers.   Pg. 57
28. Establishing a Reimbursement Plan.   Pg. 58
29. Regulating Benevolence Type Funds.   Pg. 59
30. Distributing Scholarships wisely.   Pg. 61
31. Overseeing PCUSA Mission Funding.   Pg. 62
32. Church wide Special Offerings.   Pg. 63
33. Understanding and Paying Per Capita.   Pg. 64
34. Initiating Billing when needed.   Pg. 65

Reporting

35. Regularly Reporting financial info.   Pg. 69
36. Setting the Budget and presenting it.   Pg. 70
37. Distributing Monthly Reports.   Pg. 72
38. Annual Reports for the Membership.   Pg. 73
39. Financial Activity, i.e. Profit & Loss.   Pg. 74
40. Financial Position, i.e. Balance Sheet.   Pg. 75
41. Adding Notes on the Balance Sheet.   Pg. 76
42. Understanding Fund Reporting.   Pg. 77
43. Funds with Donor Restrictions.   Pg. 78
44. Funds without Donor Restrictions.   Pg. 79
45. Treatment of Endowment Funds.   Pg. 80
46. Maintaining a Reserve Fund.   Pg. 81
47. Preparing the GA Statistical Reports.   Pg. 82

48. Preparing the Government Reports.   Pg. 83

Property, Insurance, and Personnel

49. Overseeing all aspects of the Property.   Pg. 87
50. Resource Management in the Church.   Pg. 88
51. Finding proper Insurance.   Pg. 89
52. Leasing out the Church Buildings.   Pg. 90
53. Be aware of all Personnel matters.   Pg. 91
54. Follow any approved Personnel Policies.   Pg. 92
55. Hiring and Letting People Go.   Pg. 93
56. Independent Contractor or Employee.   Pg. 94
57. Doing Payroll or Having a Payroll Co.   Pg. 95
58. Hiring Ministers and CLPs.   Pg. 96
59. Understanding Minister's Compensation.   Pg. 98
60. Understanding Total Effective Salary.   Pg. 99
61. Anticipating Financial Problems.   Pg. 100
62. Receiving Session Minutes.   Pg. 100
63. Continually Preparing for the Review.   Pg. 101
64. Resources.   Pg. 105

(Intentionally Blank)

Functions of A Church Treasurer

Practically speaking, the elected Treasurer should be the central contact for all church finances. While the Treasurer may have a team surrounding them, they become the primary point of contact and oversight in all financial areas of the church.

In the Table of Contents, you will find a list of responsibilities for the Treasurer of the church. Your church might not be doing or need to do all of these items but it would be helpful for you to be familiar with the total scope of church finances. You and as much team as you have will serve the Session as you provide the financial oversight for your church.

In states where the church is a corporation, the Treasurer of the church is usually also the Treasurer of the corporation. It is the responsibility of the Treasurer in consultation with the Clerk of Session to create or maintain a current corporation status for the church through updated filings and payment of required fees. (See *Legal Resource Manual for Presbyterian Church (U.S.A.) Middle Governing Bodies and Churches: 2010.)* Pg. 105, Resources.

The Treasurer should be prepared to attend any committee, trustee meeting, and Session meetings if invited, and also present at those meetings reports and recommendations in regard to the budget and church financial matters that pertain to that committee or group. (Be sure you communicate with the Session before you disclose information to a committee that does not directly pertain to their role.)

The Treasurer should be sure that at least one other authorized individual knows how to access all aspects of the financial information in case of an emergency need when the Treasurer is out of town or unable to continue serving for some period of time.

General Responsibilities

(Intentionally Blank)

1-Introduction to Church Finances

Many functions of the church have financial implications: offerings, budgets, stewardship programs, personnel, insurance, taxes, investments, endowments, loans, and grants are the obvious ones but programs and even worship cannot run smoothly without the financial support to make things happen. Well done, Treasurer, you have a great role to play. Hopefully, this Handbook will help you carry out the tasks with the least amount of worry.

Far too often churches elect volunteers because of their love for a person and their trust in their reputation. Love and reputation go a long way to support the volunteer but they do not provide the volunteer with the expertise and training needed to carry out the job. This Handbook should give you an easy reference to how you might carry out the specific tasks you take on as the Treasurer.

It would be impossible with one small publication to answer every question that you might have. This Handbook is a little brother to "The Church Treasurer's Manual." The Handbook will often refer you to the full document which is available as a download from Amazon books.

If you find that something is missing from the Handbook or the Manual or you would like further clarification, please contact the author, Edd Breeden by email at edd@breeden.us.

Both of these books, the Handbook and the Manual are available in online format and in printable format.

Please let us know your suggestions to make this resource better. Thank you.

2-The Financial Team

The Financial Team consists of the people who have a responsibility over the flow of money and the physical assets of the congregation; i.e. donations, bank accounts, budget, spending, buildings, etc.

This Team, regardless of how many people are involved, serve the church under the guidance of the Session/Board and should have the Session confirm and authorize all changes in policies.

The Team consists of the following functions:

A Finance Committee, designated by the Board or elders to oversee the business of the church. This might also be the Trustees of the Corporation.

A Treasurer, the point person overseeing the financial operations of the church.

The Ushers, who collect the offerings and in some form, safeguard the money until it can be passed on to the Financial Secretaries.

Financial Secretaries, those who count the money, record the giving information and deposit the money into the bank.

The Bookkeeper(s), those who record transactions in the accounting software or "books," writes the checks, and files the financial paperwork.

Building Committee or the Property Committee, the group who would be more focused on the care and maintenance of all property owned by the church.

This Team, often under the direction of the Treasurer, will be the ones who keep the financial work of the church running smoothly. They provide the basis for the internal controls in order to minimize opportunities for things to slip through the cracks.

3-A System of Record Keeping

Financial records should be as simple as possible depending upon the size of the church and its assets. The Treasurer should maintain a "filing system" of some sort that includes;

A "paper trail" of the inflow & outflow of monies,

The appropriate personnel records,

And the permanent records of financial and property transactions, including the vital information of the church; Articles of Incorporation and By-Laws.

The computer bookkeeping systems will have a record of the contributions of members and other inflow of money as well as the checks that have been written to pay the various expenses of the congregation. But beyond the computer bookkeeping system the Treasurer should maintain files related to this year's receipts and expenditures. This might include counting sheets used by the weekly Counters, deposit records including the actual deposit slip from the bank, all copies of bills and corresponding checks written and some way of keeping track of bills paid online directly from your bank. The expense files can be kept separated by months of the year or by individual vendors depending on how many checks your church writes in any given month. I personally prefer the Vendor file method because I usually have to go looking for something by the name of the vendor rather since I don't always know the particular date.

The Treasurer should file a copy of all financial reports in the church office. Other records could include the information about restricted funds; when they were given, who gave them, what they are to be used for and what happens to any monies left over.

Personnel Records should be maintained in the form of individual files for each and every employee. This file should include their date of hire and termination, wages/salary and salary changes, and all paperwork necessary for payroll including their annual W-4 or W-9 information, the I-9 identification, etc. These files should include the paperwork for annual or more often personnel reviews, copies of letters related to their performance and decisions of the Board or Personnel Committee about their status. Note: Personnel files should be kept in a locked cabinet.

Permanent Records include records of the Corporation, Articles of Incorporation, By-Laws, annual Statement of Information filings, Filings of Religious and Welfare Exemptions and Business Property Forms. In addition to Corporation paperwork, deeds of property, records of purchases, sales and upgrades of equipment, current insurance policies, bank account and loan applications, equipment manuals, leases, auto registrations, etc. These records should be kept related to any assets that will be more permanent to the church as opposed to monthly, annual, bills. Some of these permanent records can be disposed of after a number of years or when the product expires or is sold. For more information on how long to keep records you should refer to Pg. 33, How long should you Retain Records?

Permanent records should be kept in a fire/theft protected safe or a bank safety deposit box. (Be sure the Session/Board gives authority to at least two people to enter the safety deposit box, in case of one not being available when needed). The Treasurer should make sure the names of authorized people are kept current.

Vital Information should be kept in a folder under lock and key with all essential information for the church regarding the finances: (It would be helpful to keep a copy in the safe or safety deposit box off site.) ***Do not have this list in a file on your computer where it is susceptible to hacking.***

- Federal ID# and State ID#s – Tax Exempt, State Withholding #, Local Withholding #.
- Bank(s), account number(s), online ID names and passwords.
- Investment firm contact and phone # - Include any account numbers, passwords and online ids.
- Loan information – how financed, account #, rate, term, what it is secured by, payment information, etc. Include dates when started.
- Documents from all contributions of donor Restricted Funds (Pg. 78), including the name of the donor(s), the purpose of the fund, whether the principal can be used, under what conditions, how the money can be spent, the length of time the church should maintain this fund and what to do with any funds left over at the end of the fund's life.
- List of church software being used including version, serial numbers, secure passwords and support phone numbers. Update this information every time a software or password is changed.
- Copies of all equipment invoices (particularly computer equipment and copiers), including serial numbers, date of purchase, cost and warranty information.

- List of phone numbers/websites used in the Treasurer's work, bank, investment firm, local and state tax office(s).
- Any other pertinent info for your congregation.

4-Financial Policy and Procedures

Most churches function in the area of finances by the seat of their pants assuming that everyone in a position knows what they should be doing and know how to do it right. If that were truly the case, there would be little need for a Handbook like this one.

Churches should have a written set of procedures that have been approved by the Board and that are followed by every person on the Finance Team. These procedures should at the minimum include:

- Job descriptions for each person on the Finance Team.
- A Gift Acceptance Policy describing the kinds of gifts and restrictions for donations. Pg. 40.
- A Cash Disbursement Policy. Pg. 55.
- A Procedures for Counting Offerings designed to protect counters & prevent fraud. Pg. 43.
- A Conflict of Interest Policy which protects the people of your church. Pg. 31.
- *A Fully Accountable Expense Reimbursement Plan so any given expense does not become income for the recipient.* Pg. 58.

- Some practice to avoid one person doing everything, collecting, counting, depositing, writing checks and signing them.
- The need for cash receipts to be recorded and deposited in a timely fashion.
- A way to have expenses approved by a chair of the committee before the check is written.
- The use of serially numbered checks or bank records for all expenses to avoid fraud.
- The requirement of receipts for all petty cash expenditures.
- The reconciliation of all "bank" accounts each month and updated in the computer system.
- The timely entry of transactions into the computer software program to allow for accurate monthly financial reports.
- Production of Financial Reports by the Finance Committee for the Session/Board for review monthly or at least quarterly.
- The opening and review of Bank statements and cancelled checks on a monthly basis.
- Investigation of all unusual items in a timely fashion.
- A filing system that includes copies of all bank deposit receipts in a file with other financial records.
- The requirement of daily deposits or at a minimum weekly.
- Use of a budget or forecast to detect whether goals are achieved. Pg. 70.
- Incorporation of hiring policies and practices which include drug testing, background checks and contact with provided references. Pg. 92.

- A policy to have all staff, officers, and appropriate volunteers trained in "safe church practices" to prevent abuses of any type.
- Be sure to have up to date Personnel Policies. Pg. 92.
- The need for each employee to have a Job Description and receive an annual job performance review.

5-Bookkeeping

By all means, I believe churches should use some form of computer software to track their contributions and their finances. This will offer you plenty of reporting options and minimize the spreadsheets and other paper work.

Software comes in two forms: **"Accounting"** programs like ACS®, PowerChurch®, CDM® and Servant Keeper® offer you strict parameters within guidelines that make accountants happy. **"Bookkeeping"** programs like QuickBooks® or Quicken® provide a more simplified program for volunteers to work with. The choice depends on the size of your church, the number of accounts, funds, and categories you have in your budget. Most churches under 75 members can do all they need on QuickBooks® and / or Quicken®.

Contributions: Individual contributions can be easily tracked in all of the software packages except Quicken. Using another software package for tracking contributions makes sense if you are using Quicken®. Some churches prefer to use separate software to track this information and print giving reports. That really comes down to a preference in software.

Computer backups: should be made regularly. Most churches are now using cloud back-up or even cloud based programs which allow them to always have a back-up of their financial transactions.

More than one person should know the location of your backups, have access to them and know how to use them if the need arises. No one ever expects to die or move away, but it happens often enough that it is best to have a second person who can quickly access and use your software program.

6-Documentation, a Clear Paper Trail

Regardless of what bookkeeping method is used, there should be supporting documentation for each written check or processed expenditure. Ideally, before the Treasurer writes a check, the following information should be submitted. This is ideally included on the church's expenditure authorization form:

1. A copy of the receipt, bill, or invoice, related to the expenditure.
2. The name of the person or company on the check,
3. Address where the payment is to be sent,
4. The invoice number or date of bill, as appropriate,
5. The amount(s) to be paid,
6. Which budget line(s) should be charged,
7. Some explanation of the need/purpose of the expense,
8. The date of the request,
9. The name and signature of the person submitting the request.
10. The name and signature of the person authorizing payment. The person authorizing payment should never be the person or family

member of the person requesting the payment or to whom the check is made out.

Having a form for people to fill out makes it easier for the bookkeeper to pay the check and send the check to the right place. It takes a while to get people used to using a form but it does, in the long run, make the process uniform, the records more accurate, and when it comes time to do the annual review, things go far more smoothly.

7-Reconciling the Checking Account

It is desirable for a person who does not have authority to sign checks or make deposits to do the bank reconciliation. This is usually the Treasurer's responsibility to either do the reconciliation or oversee someone who does.

Since banks have different cycles you cannot always get your statement to run from the beginning of the month to the end. However, you should ask your bank if they can change your cycle so you can account more accurately for the end of the month on your monthly reporting.

Financial Software allows you to do your reconciliation easily on the computer. If you use financial software remember to regularly look for un-cleared items so you can see if checks need to be voided or reissued. The printout at the time of reconciliation should offer you a list of un-cleared checks.

You should make sure you do not have any un-cleared checks of more than three months old as you can assume people either have lost the check or decided not to cash it. Either way you would want to clear these items up regularly because un-cleared items will often skew your financial reports, especially if they include duplicate deposits or duplicate expenditures.

Reconciling serves as a mini audit along the way which might catch two payments for the same bill, new vendors receiving money who might not be appropriate and even missing deposits or payments that cleared the bank but never were entered into the computer. All of this will serve to keep your reports up to date, more accurate and will make your annual review easier.

8-Conflict of Interest

Part of the Articles of Incorporation of churches includes the fact that individuals are not allowed to directly benefit from the work of the church. This includes individuals who might be related to people in the church who benefit directly from contracts or business arrangements that are not fully above board. Hence the need to state what a conflict of interest might be and how the church prefers to handle these types of business transactions.

The persons involved most often are officers, pastors, other employees and volunteers, i.e. the treasurer, and their families. This creates some natural conflict because many smaller churches take advantage of working with family members for various church needs because the family members offer the services or products of their companies at a significantly reduced price.

A conflict of interest policy in a church does not have to say you cannot do church business with your family members. If you do business with them greater than, say, $500, the transactions should be fully disclosed before, during, and after the transaction.

A board member who knows of a conflict should tell the board before the discussion of the matter begins, remove themselves from the discussion and choose not the vote on the decision.

The real concern here goes back to the perception of those donors contribute to the church in good faith that funds will be handled with integrity. If a donor perceives their gift to the church is just to pay your family member, they might not be as willing to contribute in the future.

9-Passwords and Keys; Office Security

Church members tend to be very trusting of others. Women leave their purses all over the church, unattended. The computers are seldom under lock and key. And if there are keys, often the duplicate keys are in a cabinet and all of the members have been issued keys anyway. Think about security for your financial records and safeguards for those who handle money.

Keys to the office, and it should be locked, where the financial records are kept, should be only given to a few people in the church who need access to the area.

A box with all of the keys of the church should be locked, and just a few people should have a key or know where the hidden key is located. Hidden keys should not be in a desk drawer or at least not out in the open in the drawer. Change the location of "hidden" keys on an annual basis, at least.

Protect your computers. Secure them to the desk where possible. Protect the information with passwords to access the information and with antivirus software to prevent Identity theft or other kinds of fraud.

All software programs, especially financial information should require a Password to get in. Do not store those passwords on the computer; they should be handwritten on paper that is kept in a safe place. Change passwords at least annually.

File cabinets which house financial records should be lockable if they include personnel files and written down passwords, and fire protected if they contain important papers that cannot be readily replaced; i.e. deeds, policies, articles of incorporation, by laws, etc.

10-Suggestions for Records Retention.
(Listed alphabetically)

- Accident reports and claims.   7 years.
- Accounts payable ledgers/schedules.   7 years.
- Accounts receivable ledgers/schedules. 7 years.
- Articles of Incorporation.   Permanently.
- Internal reports (miscellaneous).   3 years.
- Audit report of accountants.   Permanently.
- Bank deposit slips.   3 years.
- Bank reconciliation.   1 year.
- Bank statements (not including canceled checks).   Permanently.
- Brokerage statements (annual).   Permanently.
- Budgets.   3 years.
- Capital stock and bond records: ledgers, transfer registers, stubs showing issues, record of interest coupons, options, etc.   Permanently.
- Cash books.   Permanently.
- Checks (canceled but see exception below).

- Checks, canceled for important payments, i.e., taxes, purchases of property, special contracts, etc. (Checks should be filed with the papers pertaining to the underlying transaction). 7 years.
Permanently.
- Contracts, mortgages, notes & leases (expired). 7 years.
- Contracts, mortgages, notes & leases (still in effect). Permanently.
- Copyright registration. Permanently.
- Correspondence (routine) with customers/vendors. 1 year.
- Correspondence (general). 3 years.
- Correspondence (legal and important matters only). Permanently.
- Deeds, mortgages, and bills of sale. Permanently.
- Depreciation schedules. Permanently.
- Duplicate deposit slips. 3 years.
- Employee expense reports. 3 years.
- Employee payroll records (W-2, W-4, annual earnings records, etc.). 7 years.
- Employee personnel records (after termination). 7 years.
- Employment applications. 3 years.
- Expense analyses and expense distribution schedules. 7 years.
- Financial statements (end of year, other months optional). Permanently.
- Freight bills. 3 years.
- Garnishments. 7 years.
- General & private ledgers (and end of year trial balances). Permanently.

- Insurance Policies (expired). 7 years.
- Insurance records, current accident reports, claims, policies, etc. Permanently.
- Internal audit reports (in some situations, longer retention periods may be desirable). 3 years.
- Inventories of materials and supplies. 7 years.
- Invoices to customers. 7 years.
- Invoices from vendors. 7 years.
- Journals. Permanently.
- Magnetic tape and tab cards. 1 year.
- Minute books for director and stockholders, including bylaws and charter. Permanently.
- Notes receivable ledgers and schedules. 7 years.
- Payroll records and summaries, including payments to pensioners. 7 years.
- Petty cash vouchers. 3 years.
- Property appraisals by outside appraisers. Permanently.
- Property records: including costs and depreciation reserves. Permanently.
- Purchase orders. 7 years.
- Retirement and pension records. Permanently.
- Savings bond registration-records of employees. 3 years.
- Stenographer's notebook. 1 year.
- Stock and bond certificates. Permanently.
- Subsidiary ledgers. 7 years.
- Tax returns and worksheets, revenue agent's reports and other documents relating to determination of income tax liability. Permanently.
- Telephone logs/message books. 7 years.
- Time cards. 7 years.

- Trade mark registrations.   Permanently.
- Training manuals.   Permanently.
- Voucher register and schedules.   7 years.
- Voucher for payments to vendors, employees, etc. (Includes allowances and reimbursements of employees, officers, etc. for travel and professional expenses).   7 years.
- Withholding tax statements.   7 years.

11-Annual Church Financial Review

The Treasurer should make provision for the church's financial records to be reviewed annually. While this review is to protect the church from some possible fraud, it also serves the purpose of helping the church improve their management of and procedures for handling financial and physical assets.

The results of said review, including any suggestions for changing future procedures, should be recorded in the minutes of the Session so the findings will be on record. This audit or financial review may be **external** or **internal**.

An external review is done by an independent auditor or an accounting firm. It is important to use someone well versed in church and clergy tax laws as well as non-profit / church finances.

An internal review is normally conducted by a committee of church members versed in accounting procedures (as long as they are not related to the Treasurer.) Some churches have partnered with other churches in their area and "traded" review committees to get the job done for less cost.

A review consists principally of looking over all aspects of the church finances and determining that the financial picture being presented to the Session and the congregation is accurate. And it often reviews the procedures and the documentation of the financial process.

The goal of the annual financial review is to look for proper accounting, guard against incidences of fraud, and other procedural errors or habits that need to be corrected in a timely fashion.

12-Financial Review Committee Checklist

As mentioned in the last section, the review committee should look at a variety of areas of both financial transactions and financial procedures. This **process should include a review:**

- **of the bank accounts,** statements, and the "books" of the church to see that accounts are reconciled regularly and each income or disbursement was handled correctly.
- **of handling of offerings** and donations; including the depositing of monies into the bank.
- **of the check writing** and cash flow, does every expenditure have the proper bill, request sheet, signatures, and been reconciled.
- **of all financial reports** distributed throughout the year, are they consistent with each other.
- **of records keeping and safeguarding** of valuable papers, including tax filings, property deeds, mortgage and insurance paperwork, etc.
- **of payroll files and processes.**
- at this time, it would also be appropriate to review **all leases, if any,** the church might have

with outside parties using the church facilities, whether they are paying rent or any payment by another name; i.e. reimbursement for utilities, donation, etc.
- **of the member contribution records.** Was the final year-end statement produced and mailed.
- **of the insurance policies** to verify the coverage and all payments.

A complete list of review items in great detail is in the Church Treasurer's Manual. See Resources. Pg. 105.

Revenues

(Intentionally Blank)

13-Cash Revenues (Income)

All monies which come into a Church should be identified in the records as to who made the gift, the amount of the gift and the nature of the gift so that the gift can be properly receipted. If the gift includes a restriction as to how it should be used, the Session should be notified before the gift is deposited unless the restriction has been previously approved by the Session. (See more information about Gift Acceptance Policies. Pg. 40 and Restricted Gifts. Pg. 78)

In general Cash Revenues (Income) are broken into six major categories which coincide with the PCUSA Annual Statistical Report. Using these categories in your accounting make finding the information easier when filling out the report.

1. **Contributions** (Cash, Check, Credit Card, Online, Stock, etc.) –This includes payments on pledges, donations from identified sources, loose offerings, stock gifts, in-kind gifts, and special offerings.
2. **Other Income** - This is all other income that does not necessarily need a deductible receipt, such as rent, sales, and tuition/fees, etc.
3. **Capital and Building Funds** - All receipts for non-budgeted capital improvement purposes.
4. **Investment and Endowment Income** – The church should define Investment and Endowment Income in their Investment Policy so it will be clear to all, exactly what is meant by "Income" on investments. See Pgs. 50, 51.
5. **Bequests** – This is income received from wills and estates, whether cash, stock, or even

property. Restrictions should be properly noted. See Pg. 76.
6. **Subsidy or Aid** – This is money received to be used in local mission and program.

14-Gift Acceptance Policy

A Gift Acceptance Policy includes information on how the Session of this church will handle all monies that come under its care. The Policy allows the Session to define some guidelines before people give money so that future misunderstandings can be minimized.

A sidelight for a moment. We all know that when someone gives money to the church they are giving it to God and they should step back and let God do what He wants to do with it through the decisions of the Session. Even the IRS questions the tax deductibility of any gift given to the church with Restrictions, strings attached, because it might not truly be "given" to the church. It might really just be pass through gift to "make it" tax deductible.

So, what goes into a Gift Acceptance Policy? Statements about what methods someone can use to give, what kinds of gifts a church is willing to receive, what is included in the General Fund expenses, what special Funds the church has already set up in case someone wants to "designate" or Restrict the use of their gift to a particular cause, what a person can do if they want to make a gift to the church for a particular cause the Session has not yet designated, what the church will do with gifts given "in memory of a loved one," how the Session has the right to refuse any gift that places undo restrictions on its use and the like. It will also state what kinds of non-cash gifts the church is equipped to accept, why the

Session might refuse a gift and what recourse a giver has to give the gift and get their wishes done.

The reason this is so big of a concern these days is that all gifts with Restrictions **that the Session accepts** must be accounted for into the future and only used for the Restricted purpose. See Pg. 78.

Churches should also be quite careful with solicited monies where a particular cause is mentioned as the money is given and the Session decides not to do the project or to use the left over money for something else. The Session should never redirect these monies for a different purpose without consulting with the original givers, their families or the Attorney General of the State. Which is good reason for the Policy so that it can be stated up front that the Session will redirect a gift after a certain number of years if the project is no longer feasible for the congregation or the project is over and there is money left in the Fund. An example; money given in the 1960s for a new organ and the church would rather spend it on new drums and guitars for the praise band. The Session needs the help of donor or the State Attorney General to make this decision.

The Gift Acceptance Policy can also specify things about the church's definition of use of the original amount given, how it interprets "income" if the fund is to be Invested (Pg. 78) and whether some of the principle amount can be spent. An example is this; some donors will designate that only the "income" can be used but the "capital" must not be spent. A Gift Acceptance Policy will help the Session clarify with the donors what is included in the working definition of "income" (i.e. interest only, dividends, capital gains, growth in value, etc.) and what is meant by "capital" (i.e. the original amount contributed, original amount and all growth, some growth, no growth.

If donors know these definitions before they give they can more comfortable accept how the monies are used.

15-Memorial Giving and Special Gifts

Memorial Giving: Often when a loved one dies the family will designate gifts to the church in lieu of flowers. The Session is the one who usually makes the decision as to what is done with the money. Once decided, the procedure can be described in the Gift Acceptance Policy for all in the church to understand what the Session will do.

Options for the Session to decide include:
--Put the money in the General Fund.
--Put the money in a special Fund spent by the Memorial Committee on capital expenditures with a lasting value; i.e. cabinets, stained glass windows, musical equipment, etc.

Special Gifts: Although many special gifts come in the form of property, stock, carpets, furniture, the Session should have a plan for how they will handle these gifts.

For instance, all stock gifts will be sold upon receipt or all property will be rented out to provide a lasting income for the youth program.

There is no right way to handle Memorial Funds or Special gifts, it just would be beneficial for the Session to make these decisions before the gift comes and communicate that to the congregation regularly.

16-Procedures for Counting Offerings.

1. Only people approved by the Session should count the offerings.
2. Two unrelated people should always process the offering to avoid any mishandling of monies.
3. Your church might choose to have only one counting team, however substitutes should be available to rotate in from time to time.
4. All offerings taken during the week should be the responsibility of the counting team. Midweek monies should be stored in a safe place.
5. The Counters need to secure their own replacements from the approved substitute list.
6. Counters who are from the same family should not serve on the same counting team.
7. Confidentiality in handling members' gifts and contributions shall be respected at all time.
8. No records shall be retained by the Counting team but shall be passed on to the Financial Secretary and the Treasurer for posting to the church's records.
9. The Treasurer should provide a set of written instructions for the Counters so things will be done in a consistent manner to assure accuracy.
10. Often the counters also fill out the contribution records in the computer.

11. The insurance coverage of the church says that all counting should be done at the church.
12. The Financial Secretary will be responsible to reconcile the amount shown on the counter's sheet as the total of the offering received with the bank deposit slip validated by the bank and the amount credited on the bank statement. The Counters will assist in resolving any discrepancies that appear.

17-Maintaining Members' Giving Records

The Treasurer with the help of a Financial Secretary should maintain a complete record of member pledges and details of their contributions to the church and church's programs. These records need to be kept in enough detail to give any donor adequate reporting for IRS tax purposes.

The IRS requires churches to list the date of each gift, the amount of the gift, and the purpose for the gift, i.e. General Fund or some other Fund. This will require a split listing when a donor gives one check and desires it to be used partly for the General Fund and partly for Benevolence.

Some churches give these statements to donors quarterly, as an opportunity to send a "thank you note" to the donors. However, all donors should receive a detailed year-end statement of their giving, again listing each gift by date, amount and purpose given.

Note: The IRS specifically excludes donations made to a tax exempt organization with the requirement that the funds go to a specific needy person. These are called "earmarked" or "pass-through" donations in which the not-for-profit organization functions as an agent of transfer rather than the recipient of the donation. In essence; the only reason that the donor made the contribution to the tax exempt organization rather than directly to the needy person was to get a tax deduction. This practice could be interpreted as tax avoidance (evasion) and is illegal for the donor and could have legal ramifications to the ministry including loss of tax exemption if the offense is deemed by the IRS as severe enough. See Benevolence Accounts, Pg. 59.

18-Data Management

With the advent of computer systems comes the possibility of churches to collect lots of data related to its membership. Some churches keep track of attendance, involvement, interests, as well as how much they give and what are some of their favorite causes.

There are many programs on the market designed to help churches keep track of members and often allow the church to change a member's address in one place and have it changed and current everywhere else on the church's computer system. This makes it very easy to mail our reminders and stewardship letters.

While the Treasurer does not have to oversee the Data Management of the church, the Treasurer or the Financial Secretary are often the first people at church to see address changes, email changes and even different phone numbers.

It is always important to reduce the number of people who can make changes to the data base while at the same time making viewing of the data base information straight forward and easy to use by the majority of the membership.

19-Contribution Receipts/Statements
(Quarterly and Annual-Year End)

The guidelines for receipts or statements issued by the Church to their donors and acceptable to the IRS as verification of deductible donations are as follows:

- The receipt or statement should include the Name and address of the church and/or be on church letterhead with the current date.
- The receipt or statement must be "contemporaneous," i.e. dated before the taxpayer files a return for the year of contribution. The annual statement sent to the contributor during the month of January fits "contemporaneous" and allows them to include the donations in their tax return preparation.
- The receipt must include the date and the amount of each "Cash" Contribution given (cash includes, cash, check, credit card, online giving, PayPal and the like). This also includes In-Kind contributions
- When a contribution is not "cash" but a donation of tangible property, a separate receipt should be given and must include the date of the contribution and a description of the property

contributed without any value placed upon it by the church. The donor must determine and justify the value.
- The church should add to the receipt or statement the following wording, if true:
  - "Any goods and services you may have received in connection with this gift were solely intangible religious benefits."

20-Bookstores, Thrift Stores
and other enterprises in the church.

When a church enters into some enterprise, whether it is leasing the property to others, selling books or donated items, or any other exchange where the church receives money like a normal business would, it may be required to report the income separately as Unrelated Business Income. See Pg. 48.

To avoid jeopardizing your tax exempt status as a church, which should be engaged in worship and related education and mission, the Treasurer should be very familiar with UBI rules and definitions so that proper accounting can be made, appropriate forms can be filed and taxes due can be paid, when needed.

Please remember that your non-profit status is based upon your activities, not on your finances or profits. Every activity, including how you raise your money should comply with the purposes of your organization; i.e. a church is formed to be involved in the worship of God and related educational and missional activities.

The 501(c)3 exemption is based on that purpose not on the fact you are "non-profit." "Non-Profit" has nothing to do with whether you have money left over at the end of the month or year, but how you raised that money and how you used that money no matter how much you have or don't have at the end of the year.

When the church starts doing things that look like "business" it could possibly be doing things that are not worship related based upon the meanings of the tax code. The Treasurer should be familiar with this area of the tax code so as to properly report any financial activity of the church which is engaged in a potential "business."

21- Unrelated Business Income

Income is "unrelated" when it comes from a regularly conducted trade or business which is not substantially related to the purpose of the non-profit organization, in this case, the church. On the IRS website (irs.gov) they use the words, "does not contribute importantly to the exempt purpose of the non-profit organization."

Many churches engage in activities to raise money and use the profits to supplement the church's budget. **UBI is defined by how you receive the money, not how the money is used.** Three tests apply for churches to check whether their activity and its income is taxable as UBI.

1. **Is this income from "the sale of goods or services?"** Are you selling something for a fee rather than providing religious benefits for a donation? A fee is not a donation, if it is required.
2. **Is this activity "regularly conducted?"** Does the church engage in this activity with a "frequency and continuity" comparable to a for profit business? It does not need to be daily since many businesses are not open every day, but is it regularly done?

3. **Is the activity "substantially related" to the religious purpose of the church?** Once again, not the that the financial proceeds are used for church activities, but is the activity by which the money is raised, itself, substantially related to the purpose of the church.

If your church engages in regular income-producing activities, you might want to talk with a Tax Professional who can help with the understanding of filing a 990 tax form with the IRS on an annual basis.

22-Stewardship

The raising of money falls under the role of the Session of the church, and is usually not assigned to the Treasurer. However, many churches ask the Finance Committee to take on this task.

My experience has shown me the job of raising money and the job of handling money requires two very different skill sets. Raising money or encouraging donors to give requires committee members who love to tell stories, talk about vision and in general get excited about what money can do for the benefit of the church. Most Treasurers and Finance Committees are not made up of these people.

Besides this, the role of Stewardship or Fund Raising in the church more rightly should be the role of teaching the congregation about the Biblical principles of God's generosity to us and our need to learn to mimic His generous nature.

The Treasurer might be asked to assist a Generosity/Stewardship Committee in providing them with historical financial data and some general information about why people give but exciting the congregation to follow God's lead and give generously requires more of a cheer leader than a record keeper like is the role of most Treasurers. (The language is a bit exaggerated to make a point and possibly help the Board understand why most Finance Committees and Treasurers find Stewardship a difficult task).

Some of the best Stewardship Programs are year round training of the congregation in the Biblical principles of handling money. How can we best help people to learn to be generous with their financial resources as God has demonstrated His generosity with us.

23-Investments

Beyond the regular operating funds of the congregation, churches often have additional monies they will not be spending in the current year. These monies, which come from a variety of sources, might be pooled together into a favorable Investment until they will need to be used.

The first pool of excess money a church might have should be put into a Reserve Fund. (Pg. 81) The recommended amount would be equivalent to 3 months of the church's annual budget.

Money the church should consider Investing is either extra money, money that will not be needed for some time or money set aside as a form of endowment to gain "interest." If the church has a sufficient Reserve Fund, then anything over that amount might be available for more long term investing. If the church has Permanently Restricted funds, where only the interest/income will be spent, then by all means invest the principle in a longer term investment with a potentially higher rate of return,

The Session has the responsibility to act as a fiduciary for the church's Assets and as such, has an obligation to balance the protection of the principal with the production of the greatest return on the Invested money.

Some churches, out of deep fear of losing money, lean to the side of protection of principle with minimal return. Some could lean toward the side of greed and seek the riskiest and highest possible return. The balance is somewhere in between.

The church would benefit from an Investment Policy (Pg. 51) so the Treasurer or Finance Committee will have the Session's guidance in all its investing.

24-Having an Investment Policy

An Investment Policy is a document approved by the Session to explain to the church, the Finance Committee and the Treasurer how the Board would like the extra resources of the church to be Invested.

The Policy will include something about the purpose of the church's investing, who is authorized to open accounts on behalf of the church and what kinds of investments can be invested in.

The Policy should describe the differences between Cash Equivalent investments, Fixed Income investments, Stock investments and any investments in Real Property for financial gain. And the Policy should define a range of limits for investing in each of these different vehicles. For example, 2-10% Cash Equivalent, 30-50% Fixed Income, and 40-65% Stock.

The Policy should also clarify for what purpose the funds can be distributed and what amount of the fund can be distributed during any given year. If the investments are balanced between stock and fixed, then a good rule of thumb is 4% annual distribution.

The Policy should define "interest" or "income" so people understand how the Session might spend from these funds. Any given investment has an annual "Return on Investment" (ROI). This is a combination of interest, dividends, long and short-term capital gains and any change in the value itself. If you add all of these "returns" together, you will have the ROI of your portfolio for the year. This is a preferred way to look at the annual "income." You do not want to spend all of the "Return on Investment" because you would like to have an increase in your principle each year to produce a slightly greater return next year.

Disbursements

(Intentionally Blank)

25-Cash Disbursements (expenses)

Cash Disbursements include all expenditures made by the church. These usually fall into 8 categories which coincide with the PCUSA General Assembly Statistical Report (Pg. 82) filed annually by the clerk with information from the Treasurer.

1. **Local Program** –These expenses usually make up the majority of the church's annual budget.
2. **Local Mission** includes all monies paid for local mission programs, ministries, and projects approved and directed by the Session/Board and/or to local ecumenical bodies.
3. **Capital Expenditures** includes all monies expended for real property or capital improvement of property.
4. **Investment Expenditure or transfers**, includes money that is newly placed into savings or investments and the related costs or fees.
5. **Per Capita Apportionment** includes the monies expended for Presbytery, Synod, and General Assembly apportionment. Pg. 64.
6. **Validated Mission PC(USA)** includes the total of all monies given for Presbyterian mission purpose including Basic Mission Support, the 4 major Special Offerings each year and any Special Appeals except for the Theological Education Fund.
7. **GA Theological Education Fund** is the voluntary amount requested of each congregation and added to your Per capita if you choose to give it.
8. **Other Mission** is the total of all monies expended for mission causes not related to the Presbyterian

Church (U.S.A.) and not already included under any of the seven items listed above.

26-Vendors

Vendors and Service Providers:
Anyone who comes on the premises to help the church maintain the buildings and grounds or to help facilitate the running of church or guest programs. (Including, but not limited to: utilities, landscapers, janitorial services, wedding service providers, caterers, photographers, maintenance crews, contractors, etc.)

The church would be well served to only hire licensed and bonded vendors for insurance purposes.

The church also would be well served to have these vendors, in all circumstances, provide the church with proof of insurance and preferably naming the church as an additionally insured. This seems like a lot of extra work until some accident happens and you have to sort out who is at fault and whose insurance will pay. If you don't have that settled ahead of time, the church might be liable for everything that happens.

Paying Vendors and Government Filings:
Because you might need to file a form 1099 for any individual or vendor at the end of the year, obtain from them a completed W-9 form before you issue to them their first check of the year. (Keep these forms in a separate file for W-9s). The first check might be less than the required filing threshold of $600.00 but when writing the first check you do not know if you will pay them again later in the year. Even if you have collected this form and information in a previous year it is good to have a new form and current information each year. Note: If your church

has a fiscal year different from the calendar year, you are obligated to send out 1099 forms based upon on calendar year payments not on fiscal year payments.

27- Checkbooks and Authorized Signers

All accounts of the church, whether checking, savings, or investment accounts, should be opened only at the direction of the Session.

The Treasurer should maintain the "checkbooks" of these accounts by receiving the statements and reconciling them monthly.

The Treasurer should not be the only signer on an account in case a check or transaction is needed when the Treasurer is ill or out of town.

It is recommended that all checks over a specific dollar amount, set by the Session, be reviewed by the Session or a designated Session member, before being signed by the Treasurer.

Authorized Signers:

Yearly, the Session should authorize persons responsible for signing checks and approving expenditures; this should be recorded in the minutes of the meeting. This would include the Treasurer and at least one other person to sign checks. And it would include a list of people, like committee chairs, clerk of Session, business manager, etc. who are authorized to approve expenditures for various committees or areas of the budget. The actual signatures of these individuals should be on record with the Treasurer's files so if there are questions at the time of the audit/review, signatures can be compared.

Church members should submit bills for reimbursement to the chair of the appropriate committee for authorization of payment. The Session can make a one-time authorization for recurring payments of mission, per capita, utilities or other expenditures in an approved budget.

28-Expense Reimbursement Plan

Provided the church has a written Expense Reimbursement Plan approved by the Session, the distributions from the church to an *employee* might not count as wages on their W-2 form. If there is no Plan or the expense does not comply with the Plan, then all reimbursements should be added to wages and put on the W-2 as taxable income. This includes *Pastor Discretionary Accounts.*

All property, goods and services purchased under this Expense Reimbursement Plan belong to the church, not the individual. In addition to the rules and regulations of the IRS, the following requirements for expense reimbursement apply:

1. Reimbursements shall be paid out of church funds and not by way of payroll deductions.
2. Original or copied receipts are required for any reimbursement of expenses and should be submitted in a timely manner defined in the Plan.
3. Requests should be submitted on proper forms & approved by someone other than the payee.
4. If the church issues a cash advance on reimbursements, the employee will properly account for the use of funds and return receipts and any excess money to the church.
5. All mileage expenses will be reimbursed at the current year IRS rate.
6. Documentation for expenses should include the receipt, the account to charge the money to, the

reason for the purchase, the persons met with, & a short summary of business topics discussed.
7. A copy of the Plan should be signed by the employee at the time of hire showing full understanding of the policy and its purpose.

29-Benevolence or Deacon's Fund

Many churches collect offerings for a Fund to help those in need. The disbursements can come in the form of gift certificates, paying for a motel room in town, paying a utility bill, buying gas, providing a meal, developing a food pantry, having a clothes closet or any number of ways to provide assistance to someone who calls or comes to the church in need. After all, this is one of the many ways we can show the love of Jesus Christ to the world. But we still need to look at the financial complications with the Benevolence or Deacon Fund, or any other creative and caring name your church has come up with.

Funding:

Funding these projects can come from Special Offerings, like the monthly appeal on Communion Sunday or just a general awareness of the church's program, letting people contribute to it.

If the funding is given for an individual or a family, the church should be careful not to be acting as a pass through agency that is just helping the donor receive a tax deduction for a gift that does not qualify for one. (Please read the rest of this section.)

Dispensing:

When it comes to dispensing the assets of the Fund to a needy person there are a few financial things for the Treasurer to keep in mind beyond the normal questions of how much might the church be enabling the needy person to continue being needy.

The Treasurer and the Session should develop guidelines for dispensing the goods and funds they have collected. Listed below are three key guidelines that should be **considered** before making a distribution:

Dispensing Guidelines:
1. **Is there a need?** This might seem obvious, especially when a homeless person arrives at the church's door, but if a neighbor comes to the church looking for help on their Electric Bill, this might be more of a valid question. Or, what if the person asking for help is a member of the congregation, what is the extent of their need?
2. **Can the person provide for that need on their own?** Do they have funds or other means to provide but they do not want to use those savings accounts at the moment so they ask the church for help?

Note: Both 1 and 2 are guideline questions that often will not have a clear answer but they should at least be considered when making the decision to dispense goods.

3. **Is this a Pass Through Contribution?** This question helps the church to avoid getting into the habit of passing contributions through to individuals which would keep the contribution from qualifying as a tax deduction.

Does the person fit in a larger "class" of people? For example, did you go around the church gathering funds for Sally because her house just burnt down? If, on the other hand, the collection was for the community good because there was a fire in the neighborhood, and anyone who was affected by the fire knows of the fund and could apply for assistance, and Sally is the only one who applied, then the potential "class" of people you could dispense to is larger than just Sally and her family.

If the "class" of people is small, i.e. members of the church, of the neighborhood, all of the seminary students in our church, etc. the gift might be a pass through rather than a legitimate tax deduction.

30-Scholarships

Since we are talking about dispensing Restricted Funds Pg. 78, let's talk a moment about funds that might have been given to the church or set up by the church for the purpose giving Scholarships to Youth, College, Seminary or even Camping Programs. These Funds also need to follow the 3 guidelines listed above under the Benevolence Fund heading. (pg. 59)
1. Does the person have a real need?
2. Do they have a way to meet that need on their own?
3. Is there a larger "class of people" that know about this scholarship and have the opportunity to apply for it?

The concerns here are the same. Are we just trying to help a person from our congregation who might or might not have a real need and do it in such a way that the donors can take a tax deduction for their gifts? If they don't need the deduction but just want the gift to be anonymous we don't have a problem, but then the gift cannot be placed on the year end statement of giving.

Note just in case you have not seen this in other places in the Handbook: The IRS treats donations made to a tax exempt organization with the requirement that the funds go to a specific person, needy or not. These are called "earmarked" or "pass-through" donations in which the not-for-profit organization functions as an agent rather than the recipient of the donation. In essence; the only reason that the donor made the contribution to the tax exempt organization rather than directly to the person was to get a tax deduction.

A Scholarship Fund, like a Benevolence Fund must be available to a larger class of people.

31 – PCUSA Mission Funding

Collection and disbursement of Funds

All monies collected for mission funding should be treated **as Funds with donor restrictions** (Pg. 78) and should not be used for any other purpose. If monies are to be sent on to the Receiving Site designated for your Presbytery, they should be sent in a timely manner; at least monthly. Too often a Treasurer waits until the last dollar comes in and then forgets to send in the money. The denomination, the programs and the individual missionaries are depending on you, the Treasurer, to send in these monies in a timely fashion.

Basic Mission Support

Your gift to shared Basic Mission Support strengthens and promotes the mission of the entire church. Your generosity will share God's Work and Words around the world through mission personnel, Christian education, evangelism, new church development and ministries with all God's children.

Directed Mission Support

Directed Mission Support are gifts given to particular programs chosen by the donor. Your gifts support PC(USA) mission co-workers, Christian education, worship and stewardship, new church development and redevelopment, Presbyterian camps, ministries in higher education and the production of resources and services to strengthen congregations.

As people of God's mission, Presbyterians are making a difference as we carry God's word and works to all His children.

32-Church-wide Special Offerings

There are four church-wide special offerings during the year: see http://specialofferings.pcusa.org.

- **One Great Hour of Sharing** is taken during the Easter Season as an "ecumenical effort to alleviate the effects of poverty, injustice, and disaster." (32% for Disaster Assistance; 36% for the Hunger Programs; and 32% for Self-Development of People)
- **Pentecost** is taken during the season of Pentecost to address the needs of at-risk children and young people. (40% Youth Work in churches; 25% Young Adult Volunteers; 25% Youth Ministries; and 10% advocating for Children-at-Risk.)
- **Peace and Global Witness** is taken in October, the season of Peace, "uniting congregations in sharing the Peace of Christ and promoting reconciliation and peacemaking within cultures of violence and conflict." (25% for responding to conflict in our communities; 25% for connecting mid-councils for Peace work; and 50% for advocating for Christ's peace and justice throughout the world.)

- **Christmas Joy** is taken in the season of Advent and Christmas "to assist church workers in their time of need and providing for the education and leadership development of our church's future racial ethnic leaders." (50% for Assistance Programs of the Board of Pensions; and 50% for racial ethnic leadership development)
- **Also note:** the denomination makes Other **Specific Appeals** for funding including the **Theological Education Fund, the Special Disaster Assistance, and Appeals through the Presbyterian Women association**.

33-PerCapita

"*Per capita* funding is how Presbyterians mutually share the costs of coming together to discern the Spirit's leading for the future." That is the opening line of the web page of the PC(USA) statement on per capita. (http://www.pcusa.org/percapita)

What is per capita?

In essence: Per capita is a set amount of money (an apportionment) per member paid by their congregations to fund the budgets of their Presbytery, Synod and the General Assembly.

At the writing of this edition the expectation of the denomination is that the Presbytery will pay the full assessment regardless of what the churches pay.

How is the per capita rate set?

Each Council sets the per capita rate by dividing their total budget for the coming year by their total membership figure that was reported in the previous year. Keep in mind, if your membership numbers are not up to date, you could be paying per capita on members you had years ago but no longer have today.

General Assembly Per Capita Budget

The per capita budget of the General Assembly principally provides for the cost of holding GA meetings, expenses of the permanent and special committees of the General Assembly, The Presbyterian Historical Society, the work of the Moderator of the General Assembly, the Office of the General Assembly, GA Publications, and some other miscellaneous expenses. Additional work in the denominations is paid for through other forms of funding.

34-Billing

The Treasurer takes on the responsibility to send out bills to others from time to time as needed. Your church might never need to send bills to people but if you do, it becomes the Treasurer's responsibility.

Some churches do their stewardship with a pledge system. While reminding a donor of their pledge and how much they have paid on said pledge is not technically a bill, it is something the Treasurer has to initiate and send to those who have pledged. Your church might have a tradition of how often to send these reminders but if not, you should set a schedule that works for you and stick to it.

Your church might send bills to the members each year for their annual Per Capita payment. Even though most churches include Per Capita as a line item in their budget, they also include per capita payments as income. Why not encourage everyone to "pay their bill;" i.e. the cost of being a member?

You might need to prepare bills for other situations like costs for weddings, cost for building use, cost for Sunday School study books, special seminars, and other items. While the church is not in the business of selling goods, it might from time to time need to send out a bill to someone. That becomes the role of the Treasurer.

Reporting

(Intentionally Blank)

35-Financial Reports

The Treasurer not only oversees the financial records of the church but is responsible to report this information to various groups in the church. Usually, this is the Session, often it is a Committee, and at least annually it is the Membership of the congregation as they are considering their giving for the coming year.

Financial reports presented to the board and the membership must be understandable to the person who does not normally think and comprehend the world of charts and numbers. So the Treasurer should be prepared to train the Session and the congregation to read the reports that are generated by the financial software. For years, I tried to restate the financial data to make it more understandable, but I have come to the opinion that training is worth the time spent.

The Basic Reports;

The Statement of Financial Activity (also called the Profit and Loss Statement; Pg. 74) is a report that lists the Revenue and Expenses for a given period of time; last month, year to date, or the whole year. This report can also show a comparison to the budget for the same period or for the whole year.

The Statement of Financial Position (also called the Balance Sheet; Pg. 75) lists all of the Assets of the church as well as the Liabilities. This is where you will see how much money is in each bank account, investment account, and the value placed on buildings and other capital assets. When notes are attached, the "Positions" are not only stated, but clarified as well.

These two reports help the board and the congregation see the complete financial situation of the church on any particular date.

36-Setting the Budget and Presenting it

Setting it – developing the line item budget.

The Treasurer may assist in the preparation of the church budget. While showing the source of monies the budget also spells out the way the church plans to spend that money on ministry. It must be both realistic and mildly flexible.

Those who prepare the budget do need to decide if their budget is a limit on spending in each area of the budget or a guess at the time of preparation. The Treasurer will want to know this, in order to flag items that are going over the spending "limit."

You could see the budget as an expression of the goals of a congregation translated into dollars and aligned in some kind of priority. Since the expected income often is unknown at the time of the budget process, it is prudent to encourage close scrutiny of both new and on-going programs.

When the budget is properly developed, continually updated, and effectively used, many beneficial results are realized such as:
1. Reduced emotional spending.
2. Improved impact of mission dollars.
3. Avoidance of unintentional diversion of dollars to lower priority causes.
4. Increased congregational participation and commitment.
5. Monitored spending.
6. Rational adjustment to meet unexpected situations.

The effectiveness of a budget in the long run depends upon two factors: the thoroughness of the planning upon which it is developed and the diligence with which it is adhered to.

Presenting it – using a Narrative Budget;

Since most members are not accountants or familiar with line item budgets, many churches have gone the next step and developed a Narrative budget. This serves as a non-accountant's tool to communicate the costs of the program of the church to the congregation. Please choose the best report format for the audience you have; i.e. hand out the Narrative Budget but also have available a line item budget for those that might prefer seeing it in the old format.

Narrative budgets effectively represent the witness of your congregation by providing a clearer picture of the mission and ministry realized through your church's offerings.

For example, the line-item budget for your congregation may show very little funding for worship. But is that accurate? A narrative budget takes all the costs for all aspects of anything related to worship and shows the real amount of the budget directed toward worship. The percentage of the minister's time that is spent in preparation and leadership of worship, the cost of utilities for worship, the cost of paper for worship bulletins, the cost of musicians as well as music directors, and music for the choir and custodial time are all a part of the real cost for Christian worship in a congregation.

The narrative budget often results in an increase in giving. People know how their money is being used to help others. They want to be a part of the vision the congregation has set. When members of your congregation see that their budget addresses real needs in the lives of people, and that their involvement and contributions are of significant value in supporting such mission, they are more likely to be generous in their giving.

37-Monthly Reporting

Each month the Treasurer should prepare a report for the Session that gives them at least a short version of the financial situation of the church, i.e. the Statements of Financial Activity (Pg. 74) and Position (Pg. 75). Depending on the financial situation of the church the Session might also want a more detailed breakdown of the income and expenses and the value of various Funds. Usually, the two main financial statements will be enough.

Your Committees might also like to have a monthly recap of the inflow and outflow of the budget lines that fall under their oversight. If this information is matched to budget, they will know what they have left to spend and can more appropriately plan for their upcoming needs.

If your team includes a Finance Committee, they might like the reports in more detail than the Session so they can do "auditing-on-the-go" by seeing discrepancies along the way and by making corrections in a timely fashion, rather than waiting until the end of the year Review of the books.

For instance, a mission committee could have chosen to stop sending money to a particular missionary who has left the field, and the Treasurer not knowing this has continued to send the monthly check. It would be better to find this out after one month than after 6 months. The same would be true if the janitorial company had been replaced and the

Treasurer had not been told. Or if the income has been lagging behind the expenses for a few months and the Finance Committee feels a need to notify the Session about possibly cutting staff or other expenses.

38-Annual Reporting to the Membership

All Presbyterian Churches are required to have an Annual Congregational Meeting and most have this meeting in the first part of the year where the committees give their summary reports for activity during the previous year. The Treasurer often presents the Statements of Financial Activity (Pg. 74) and Position (Pg. 75) as well as the Budget for the coming year. These reports should have all of the Notes (Pg. 76) attached so that members know the details of the financial situation of the church. This gives them an opportunity to ask questions and express concerns.

These Annual Reports often include a comparison to the previous year's amounts so people can see the progress or the potential setbacks that might be coming. I.e. they might see a down trend in revenues for the church from the preceding year. Or they might notice a significant increase in value of one of the funds, causing them to ask a question about either the investments or how many people contributed to making the fund rise in value.

Members who are more familiar with financial reporting in For-Profit Corporations might want to know about the different assets held by the congregation, how these might be invested, what the Return of Investment (ROI) was for the preceding year, what restrictions are placed on funds being held for specific purposes and what is the time line, if any, placed on using the funds before they revert to another use.

For more information, see Notes. Pg. 76.

39-The Statement of Financial Activity
(Often called the Profit and Loss statement)

This statement is one of the many standard reports in most all financial software. It is designed to show the "activity" or flow of money into or out of the church's accounts. The simplest of all statements of financial activity (*in italics below*) was the old method of the Treasurer's report to the Session;

Month's Beginning Balance	*$ 3,567.00*
Revenue for the Month	**2,030.00**
Expenses for the Month	**1,925.00**
Balance at the End of Month	*3,672.00*

A report like this does give a picture of the finances of the church; you see the amount of money that came in and the amount that went out. And in some small churches this might still be enough information from time to time. But most Sessions and congregations today would like to see more detail; like what is the breakdown of the revenue and the expenses so they can see how much money is coming from what sources and how much is being spent on what kinds of activities.

Revenue can be broken down by the types of income the church might have and how much detail the Session might want; pledges, loose offering, special projects, et. There is no right way to break down these categories, it truly depends on what information the Session considers helpful.

Detailed expense reports are available on most computers for the Treasurer to breakdown a category and print out a list of all of the expenses in the category; say, the music and worship expenses. It would be helpful from time to time to give this breakdown to the person(s) in charge of spending these monies so they verify the accuracy.

40-The Statement of Financial Position
(Often called the Balance Sheet)

This statement lists all of the Assets of the church as well as the Liabilities. This is where you will see how much money is in each bank and investment account, and the value placed on buildings and other capital assets. You will also see what liabilities the church might have, such as outstanding loans, bills that need to be paid, credit card balances and even the details of the Funds with or without Restrictions.

The simplest of all statements of financial position (*in italics below*) was the old method of the Treasurer's report to the Session;

Beginning Checking Balance	***$ 1,567.00***
Beginning Savings Balance	***1,005.00***
Value of the Taylor Youth Fund	***1,100.00***
Total Assets, No Liabilities	***3,672.00***

A report like this does give a picture of the finances of the church; you see the amount of money that was in the various different accounts at the end of the month. And you see there are no liabilities at the moment. And in some small churches this might still be enough information from time to time since they might not have many different accounts. But churches with numerous checking, savings, and investment accounts will need more detail.

Dividing out the Funds that have donor Restrictions, Pg. 78 and those that do not have donor Restrictions, Pg. 79 will be helpful as well as adding Notes Pg. 74 to the report that clarify the use of the Funds and maybe some deadlines to spending that are coming up. If your church does have one or more loans, the Statement of Position will show the current debt balances as well.

41-Notes on Reports

How many times have you heard someone say, "When was that money given to the church and do we have restrictions on how we can use it?" These details are expected to be tacked on to the Statement of Financial Position (Pg. 75), as they are needed.

The "Note" for each Fund should list the donor (either a single person, a larger group, or the Session) who made the Restriction, the date of the Restriction, what portion of the Fund can be used (i.e. the principal and income, just the income, or some other specific instruction), the purpose of the Fund (how it can be used), the date or circumstance when the Restrictions will be lifted for some reason, and what the Session can do with the remaining money at the time the Restrictions are lifted. This information should be gathered at the time the gift is made, but if it is an old gift, the Treasurer might need to put what is known in the Notes with an asterisks stating that information is lacking.

Under the liabilities section of this report you should have two major sections for Funds; Funds with Donor Restrictions and Funds without Donor Restrictions. These two categories are covered in more depth on Pg. 78 and 79. Simply put, when you set money aside for a specific purpose, the money fits into three different categories;

> Money that can be used anytime and anyway the Session chooses;
> Money that the Session has chosen to set aside for a specific purpose; and
> Money that the Session accepted as a gift from a donor that is earmarked for a special project.

42-Fund Reporting

A "Fund" is a pool of money that is used for a particular purpose. Funds without Restrictions usually end up in the Operating Fund, sometimes called the General Fund. If the church has a surplus of Revenue over Expenditures, I would encourage the Session to set up a Reserve Fund. Pg. 81. Once the Reserve Fund is "fully funded" the church can move to having Investments as well.

When the Session chooses to set monies aside for a specific purpose, the funds are said to be Restricted (often called designated). This means the money cannot be used for anything other than the Restriction, at least until the Restriction is removed. The Session can only remove the Restriction on Funds they have set aside for a specific purpose. If the money came to the church as a gift with a donor's Restriction and the Session accepted the gift with the Restriction, they or even future Sessions cannot change the use of the Fund. Even if the Session solicits monies from the congregation for a specific cause, the Fund has donor Restrictions.

All Restricted Funds, those with Donor Restrictions and those without Donor Restrictions should have a note associated with the Fund on the Statement of Financial Position (Pg. 75). The Note should keep the Donor and the intent of the Fund before the congregation for as long as the Fund is listed on the report.

Reporting these Funds as Liabilities allows the church to pool all of these funds into an Investment portfolio for greater tracking of investments and a better return on investment.

43-Funds with Donor Restrictions

A Fund becomes a Fund with Donor Restrictions in two ways. One, the Session accepts money from a Donor who gives the money to the church with a set of Restrictions for its use. Two, the Session could solicit money from members for a particular purpose, when the gifts come in, the Donor expects the Session will honor the stated purpose. Most States have laws governing Restricted Funds and say the money can only be used for the intended purpose. Often leaving the hands of the Session tied because they have money left over in the Fund that they can no longer use because the stated purpose is no longer needed.

A Gift Acceptance Policy, Pg. 40, will, in most cases, resolve the dilemma of Restrictions if it includes a paragraph of what the Session will do with Restricted Funds that cannot be used for the intended purpose within a reasonable amount of time. At that time the Restriction will be repurposed towards another stated purpose, chosen by the Session.

Whenever a Donor gives a check for a purpose other than a few main causes the Session has previously set up, the Session should attempt to negotiate with the Donor to at least pick a few alternative uses if the project they have in mind does not materialize. If the donation comes by way of a will and the church cannot negotiate with the Donor, the Donor's family can help with some adjustments as the church receives the money.

If the church has money on the books that has been there a long time and no one remembers the Restrictions, the Session should do research and make a determination as to the purpose and the term of the Fund.

44-Funds without Donor Restrictions
(but may have Session designations)

Gifts without Restrictions include any gift given to the Church where there is no accompanying restriction placed on the purpose or time or duration of the use of the gift, other than that it be used for purposes consistent with the tax exempt purposes of the church. Whether the gift comes directly from a living individual or through an estate settlement the Session can decide how these gifts will be used.

Since they have no Restriction the Session will make a decision about the funds; if they should just go into the Operating Fund or deposited into some other Fund Account or Investment. These monies will be accounted for in the Funds without Restrictions section of the Balance Sheet. They can be used by the Session for any reason they choose consistent with the exempt purposes of the church.

The Session has the opportunity to "designate" some of the Funds without Restrictions for specific purposes and the Treasurer will set these amounts aside in a Liability Fund with an appropriate name. The money is still classified as Funds without Restrictions because the Session can change the designation or "Restriction" at any time; the Funds are only temporarily Restricted. If, however, the Session sets these monies aside and asks members to add additional money for the project, then the whole Fund becomes a Fund with Donor Restrictions as mentioned in the last paragraph.

When the Session feels a Fund without Restrictions has run its course, they can choose to un-restrict, the monies in these funds where the Session was the only one to add a Restriction to the use of funds.

45-Endowment Funds

Many churches are used to the terminology of Endowment Funds. Endowment usually means money set aside for use as an income generator and only the proceeds will be used for specified causes which may include the Operating budget of the church.

In actuality, an Endowment is just another name for a Donor Restricted Fund or a board designated Fund without Restrictions.

Further clarification on Funds is then needed as to whether the Fund is a Permanently Restricted Fund or just Temporarily Restricted. The Treasurer can know this by the documentation which came with the gift itself or which was developed by the Donor and Session or Treasurer at the time of the gift.

You may continue to use the term Endowment if you choose but I would suggest that you remain consistent in how you use that term, if you have some Endowments that are temporary and some that are permanent, you might try limiting the word Endowment to Permanently Restricted Funds and use other names for any Fund without Donor

Restrictions or Funds with Temporary Donor Restrictions.

When working with Restricted Funds, anything other than Operating Funds, the Treasurer should make every effort to set a timeline for the Fund, stating when the Fund will become Un-Restricted and what will happen to the remaining funds when that date arrives. This information should be included in the Notes, Pg. 76, at least on an annual basis when the Treasurer reports the Financial Position, Pg. 75, of the congregation to the membership of the church at the Annual Meeting.

46-Reserve Funds

Most churches do not think about Reserves but it would be important for your church to begin to put some money in a separate Bank, Savings, or Investment Account where the money could be quickly retrieved if the need arises. Call this the Reserve Fund.

A Reserve Fund includes monies available in a time of low income or crisis. If a church has investments but does not have the Reserve Fund as a buffer, they might have to sell securities at an inappropriate time to gather cash for the need. Many churches just carry a large balance in the checking account. If it were moved to another accessible account with a little interest, it would make more sense for the church.

The checking account's operating level does not need to be more than one month's budget. This would allow you to have enough money to cover 1-2 months of low offerings, usually during the summer months. If you have two months in a row that are low, you should then withdraw monies from the Reserve Fund.

The Reserve Fund should then be an account that is available, when needed, and would have between three (3) and six (6) months' worth of the Monthly Budget. Make sure these monies could be available within 3 to 5 days if you need them.

There is no way to plan for every crisis that will come along for a church, but having a Reserve Fund that the church can fall back on in their time of need would be very comforting for the Session as they go about their regular work. The Reserve Fund would be a Fund without Restrictions because it would be money "designated" by the Session for this purpose.

Replenish the Reserve Fund as soon as your checking account reaches its operating level.

47-General Assembly Statistical Report

Annually, the Clerk of Session is asked by the Clerk of Presbytery to fill out the Annual Statistical Report from the General Assembly. These reports can now be filled out online. The Clerk will need certain financial data to fill out this report and will most likely come to the Treasurer and ask for that data. Knowing ahead of time what is needed can make the Treasurer's job a little easier.

Some churches actually build their Chart of Accounts around these required numbers for reporting or some software packages allow you to develop special reports that give you the numbers you need. I have listed Revenues, Pg. 39, and Disbursements, Pg. 55, according to the numbers you will need to fill out the Statistical Report. Setting up your accounts in these categories will give you subtotals for these reports and will it easier to fill out the report when the time comes.

Remember the report is looking for ballpark figures for the purposes of comparing changes from year to year. This means you should round your numbers to the hundreds of dollars rather than listing dollars and cents.

The categories requested might not be the same as your budget delineation; feel free to move your monies around a bit to fit the GA report, however, move things around in the same way each year for a more accurate comparison report.

This report helps the denomination with their statistics, helps your Presbytery review the overall financial situation of the Presbytery, and it helps at the time of pastoral transition, giving those pastors seeking to be your pastor some additional information about you and your history.

48-Governmental Reporting

The Treasurer is responsible to comply with community, state and federal regulations with respect to filing payroll tax reports such as the 940's, 941's, W-2's, W-3's, 1099's, 1096's and any State equivalents, etc. This includes the completion of Form 941 at least quarterly if not monthly or semi-weekly and payment of taxes withheld from payroll in the form of payroll tax deposits (Consult IRS Circular E for more information).

State and local tax codes determine the forms to use, the method of payment and the frequency. You should contact your local and state tax offices for the most current and accurate information on what you need to file and pay and when it might be due. Most of the Federal and State forms for filing payroll related taxes can be found, filled-out and filed online.

Since payroll tax can be confusing, the Treasurer might seek to hire a payroll company, which can, for a fee, produce your payroll checks and file all of your payroll related governmental paperwork for you. Since each state's regulations will differ, you might want to contact a Tax Professional in your community to help you in complying with governmental filings.

The Treasurer is also responsible for any other IRS filings such as Form 990, tax return for not for profit entities. Your church may or may not be required to file a Form 990 because of the exempt status of churches at the time of this update. However, the Treasurer should be familiar with this form or have a tax preparer who is. Check to see if your church has any Unrelated Business Income, Pg. 48, which might trigger a need for you to file this form or at least the 990EZ or 990T.

Property, Insurance and Personnel

(Intentionally Blank)

49-Property as an Asset of the Church

The value of all property owned by the church should be added to the Statement of Financial Position, the Balance Sheet. Pg. 75. The rationale for including building cost and depreciation on the balance sheet helps the organization know the cost basis of the property at the time of any future sale to determine and account for any gain or loss (usually for tax purposes). Churches don't ever think about the sale of the property since they expect to be around forever. So most churches do not include this.

The cost of the property should be listed as an asset under long term assets. This is either the actual amount paid for the property, if known, or an estimate of the value of the property when you place it on the Balance Sheet. You would also add any major (over $5,000) capital expenditures made to the facilities over time. All future leasehold improvements should be listed separately as they occur and depreciated over the life of the improvement.

The property should probably be seen as a 30-year depreciation (MACRS) and that amount should be listed as a negative number accumulating each year so you have a net value, i.e. cost basis refigured each year on the Statement of Financial Position. Pg. 75

As well as these numbers being tracked in the Statement of Financial Position, it would be good to add notes to the report if the property is ever used as collateral for loans or other obligations. These notes should include the nature of the loan, the amounts involved, as well as the dates when the encumbrance will be freed up. This is just to help the membership better understand the financial picture. Also include any other information that might be lost over time.

50-Resource Management

Physical Assets

The physical assets of the congregation must be safeguarded and maintained. Any buildings of the church must be maintained in good condition to protect the property from deterioration due to neglect.

The Building Committee or Trustees might have this responsibility but the Treasurer should be involved in the process so that bills get paid on time.

Cash Assets

Cash Assets need to be adequately managed, including opening and closing accounts when appropriate, transferring money between accounts, acquiring CDs or other investments when needed, etc. When the Treasurer sees the balances of an account going above the required expectation or below it, as well, he/she should make the appropriate adjustments. Remember to seek Session approval when needed.

Keys, Accounts and Passwords

The Treasurer has the responsibility to safeguard any keys related to financial offices and paperwork, account numbers, passwords, etc. and to be certain that only authorized persons have access to funds and official records. However, at least one other authorized person than the Treasurer (appointed by the Session and not related to the Treasurer) should know the location of necessary keys, account numbers, log in IDs, passwords, etc. As often as the Treasurer sees fit, or whenever the Treasurer is replaced with another person, the passwords and key or at least location of the "hidden" keys ought to be changed to protect the assets of the church.

51-Insurance

Churches are directed by the *Book of Order*, G-3.0112 to "obtain property and liability insurance coverage to protect its facilities, programs, staff, and elected and appointed officers."

The Session should review the adequacy of the insurance policy on an annual basis. The Treasurer should notify the Session of this need before paying the renewal fee for the church's policy. Giving the Session the opportunity to switch companies if desired.

The Treasurer should encourage the Session to choose an insurance company that has experience in "church property and program" insurance so the church is adequately covered for buildings, property, transportation, liability and programs of the congregation. It is very easy to want to search for the lowest price, since insurance is a large expense, but at the time of a claim, the church will want the best.

Remember to cover your vehicles and comply with all transportation laws about who can drive and what licenses they need. Keep appropriate logs in your vehicles and have the vehicles regularly maintained.

Those in your congregation who handle money on a regular basis should be Bonded. This is a form of insurance that covers their handling of monies and protects them and the church from issues related to fraud. This is usually a part of a Master Policy for churches, but the Treasurer should verify this.

Risk management and insurance coverage should be a high priority of the Session/trustees who have responsibility over the program and facilities of the church. Do not just hope that your policy covers your needs. Seek competent advice!

52-Leasing Out Your Church Property

More and more churches are leasing out a portion of their facilities to gain some additional income. Two concerns have to do with whether the leasing to others jeopardizes your Property Tax Exemption and whether the rental income falls under the category of Unrelated Business Income, Pg. 48. Be familiar with the rules related to UBI.

Why the church needs a Lease Agreement with all Third Party users of the church property?

A church is exposed to liability potential (accidents, injury, damage, theft, etc.) anytime a third party (vendor, service provider, individual, or organization) comes onto the church's grounds. Whether or not the church created the conditions which resulted in the injury, the church and their insurance company might find themselves in court. Proper steps, including lease agreements can help to alleviate the church's liability in these situations.

Who is a third party?

Vendors and Service Providers – anyone who comes on the premises to help the church; (Including, but not limited to: landscapers, janitorial services, wedding service providers, caterers, photographers, maintenance crews, contractors, etc.) Note: Contractors should be licensed and bonded.

Individuals or Organizations – anyone who uses space for meetings, parties, and events. (Including, but not limited to: schools, pre-schools, tenants, people renting your parking lot, other churches, community and neighborhood organizations, support groups, mission projects, book clubs, ceremonies, receptions, concerts, etc.)

53-Personnel

Most employers are affected by the Civil Right Act of 1964 (Title VII), as amended, which bans discrimination based on race, color, religion, sex or national origin in employment. There are other laws prohibiting discrimination against handicapped persons or veterans. Depending on the size of the employing organization, there are laws which pertain to hiring and firing an employee. A full list of these laws is included in the resource, *Legal Resource Manual for Presbyterian Church (U.S.A.) Middle Governing Bodies and Churches.* (Resources, Pg. 105).

The Session has the responsibility to manage the church wisely and this includes the employment of non-ordained staff, with concern for equal opportunity employment, fair employment practices, personnel policies, and the annual review of the adequacy of compensation for all staff and employees. The employment process is usually handled by a Session Authorized Personnel Committee. Refer to *Session Personnel Committee Guidelines* and also *Your Church: Employer and Small Business* available from the Insurance Board. (Resources, Pg. 105).

The Treasurer will be the person responsible for all employees to be paid on time according the amounts set by the Session in the annual budget and according to the personnel laws in your State and local. Every employee should have a separate personnel file which includes basic data; date of hire, starting wage, W-4 form (updated annually), copies of annual reviews, and other pertinent information. These files should be kept under lock and key.

54-Developing a Personnel Policy Manual

As an employer, a congregation, should develop and approve written personnel policies. While the policies may suit the unique needs of the congregation, it is important that such policies be in writing and communicated to all employees and other concerned persons.

Personnel policies should include such topics as:
- a. Compensation Policy - establishing salary ranges for each position. These policies should also cover such employee benefits as:
    1. Pension Consideration, either Pension Plan or 403b plan.
    2. Health Care Availability and Premium Assistance.
    3. Social Security and Medicare deductions and payment.
    4. Life Insurance coverage and additional options.
    5. Vacation Accrual or Award and Use.
    6. Holidays Designated.
    7. Days off Guidelines.
    8. Parental and Family Leave rules.
    9. Sabbatical and Educational Leave rules.
    10. Sick Leave rules of procedure and amount.
- b. Employment Policies.
    1. Relationship and behavior policies.
    2. Conflict of Interest Policy.

3. Equal employment/Non-discrimination Policy.
4. Whistle blower Policy.
5. Grievance process.
6. Office hours & access.

55-Hiring and Letting Staff Go

It is appropriate for the church to require job applications to be in writing before a person is considered for hire. The application would include a work history, strengths and weaknesses, and character/work references. All references should be checked before a person is hired.

In hiring a new staff person, it would be helpful for the interviewers to consider the personality traits of the interviewee and how that person will get along with the other staff they will be working with.

A Job Description should be developed for every job and reviewed again at the time of any new hire. Based on the Job Description the interviewers should be able to determine if the candidate has the qualifications needed for the job.

In is important to adhere to the Policies of the church when working with staff and their illnesses, time off, vacations, and the like. Without a firm policy and good files, it is easy for the church to be taken advantage of. Often, because the people of the church exhibit compassion, they tend to let staff stretch out illnesses with pay or excessive time off. Etc.

Be sure to follow all of the laws of your State when terminating a staff person.

56-Independent Contractor or Employee

The question always comes up as to whether you call a worker an Employee or an Independent Contractor. That question can be complicated and crucial. An Employee costs you money for payroll taxes and worker's compensation insurance and you send them a W-2 at the end of the year. An Independent Contractor doesn't require you paying their payroll taxes and you send them a 1099 at the end of the year if you have paid them more than $600 total from January to December.

Here is my quick definition to determine which a worker is:

Do you tell them when to come to work?
Do you tell them what to do?

Then they are an employee. Otherwise they could be an Independent Contractor.

Many churches, for years, have paid music personnel, Sunday child care workers and the like as if they were ICs. But you tell them to come on Sunday at 9 am and you direct how they do their job. In most cases, they are employees and should be paid as such.

If the personnel are determined to be employees by the State Employment Agency, then you might be liable for back tax penalties which are very steep.

57-Payroll

The payroll process has a number of steps:

Setting up the employee's personnel file with the I-9 form, W-4 form, a copy of their application and information about hiring and wages.

Note: you can use the IRS web service called e-verify to check on a person's Social Security number and their right to work.

Before payday, you will gather from all hourly employees and all regular Independent Contractors, a time card for the period and have someone in authority verify their time card.

Calculate their pay and figure any taxes that need to be withheld and matched by the employer.

Write the checks or set things up for direct deposit into their bank accounts.

Send in the withheld payroll tax and the matching employers taxes to the bank.

File the Monthly IRS form and the Annual summary form.

From my stand point, it is much easier to have a payroll service do most of this work. All you would need to do then is set up a new employee, enter their hours worked for the pay period and let the payroll company do the rest.

58-Hiring Ministers or Commissioned Lay Pastors

Many of the items in the Personnel Policy, Pg. 92, apply to clergy. However, listed below is some specific information about Ministers or Commissioned Lay Pastors.

1. Remember that all installed ministers must be a member of the Board of Pensions (BOP) which provides health insurance, pension and death/disability coverage. The cost of this insurance is set by the BOP each year. Consult the BOP website, www.pensions.org, for current information.

In addition to the basic coverage required for installed ordained Presbyterian Pastors, there are some optional forms of insurance available; dental, optional death/disability coverage, etc. from BOP and may be paid by the member or negotiated in the terms of call.

2. You must submit completed Member Change Forms to the Board of Pensions at the time of hire and each December until the minister no longer works for the church. This form includes changes in address of the Minister, changes in the terms of call, and changes in the electives the Minister might have.

3. Ministers are considered "Self-Employed" for Social Security Tax Purposes and are considered an "Employee" for Federal Tax Purposes. The church is not required to withhold taxes, either Social Security, Medicare, or Income, from the ordained minister's wages. If the minister files a W-4 form with the church and asks to have "additional taxes" taken out of the paycheck to help cover their tax burden at the end of the year, the church should do so. However, if the church has no other employees and does not normally file payroll forms and taxes they should encourage the minister to pay their own estimated taxes quarterly as other self-employed tax payers do.

4. How does the minister pay taxes if they don't have deductions from their paycheck? The minister is personally responsible for self-employment taxes (15.3% of wages) rather than the employer withholding social security and Medicare (7.65%) from the minister's pay and the employer paying an equivalent share (7.65%) of social security and Medicare like they do for non-ordained employees. The minister is responsible for paying self-employment taxes at the time of filing form 1040 with the IRS.

However, the ordained minister is treated as an employee when it comes to paperwork. The Treasurer or the payroll company will send/give to the minister before January 31st a form W-2 to report wages for the previous year. On the W-2 form the church will report all wages, salary, un-receipted allowances, Social Security Offset, etc. given to the pastor in Box 1 and report any housing allowance separately in Box 14.

Note: A Presbyterian Church Treasurer must look at a Pastor's Compensation in different ways depending upon what you are trying to do.
1. For tax purposes the minister is self-employed and does not have any taxes withheld from their paycheck.
2. For tax filing purposes the minister is an employee and receives a W-2 form.
3. For Board of Pension purposes the church pays certain insurance and medical fees based on a number called the Total Effective Salary.

59-Minister's Compensation Package

Compensation Categories: The Pastor's Compensation Package fits into four major categories.

Salary, this portion of Compensation will be treated as taxable income, subject to Self-Employment taxes (SECA). This is not just the wages but any additional un-accounted for reimbursements; bonuses, retirement contributions, and extra life insurance.

Housing Allowance, this portion of Compensation, when designated ahead of time by the Session of the church, will be treated as non-taxable income; it is not reported on the W-2 in box 1. It will be subject to the SECA taxes when the minister files a Form 1040 tax return. The minister can ask the Session to set this number up to 100% of their Compensation but they must justify the expenses of the housing costs on their tax return for the total amount of Housing to remain non-taxable income.

Expense Reimbursements, this portion of Compensation are allowances which the church pays to the pastor under a Fully Accountable Reimbursement Plan Policy. Pg. 58. The accountable portion of Compensation will be treated as non-taxable income, it is not subject to the SECA taxes and consequently will not be reflected on the pastor's W-2; it is considered employer paid benefits. If the pastor does not account for the expenses they should be added to the wages in box 1 of the W-2 form at the end of the year.

Fringe Benefits. this portion of Compensation made up of expenses that can be legally sheltered as a tax-free benefit. This portion of Compensation will be treated as non-taxable income, and not subject to the SECA taxes.

60-Total Effective Salary

The Board of Pensions calculates the amount owed by the church for the Medical and Pension dues off of a number they call the **Total Effective Salary.** This number is similar to the Minister's Compensation with a few adjustments.

Salary; the Total Effective Salary is the total amount of salary used for the Wages, Box 1 of the W-2, minus the amount of compensation separated to pay the Social Security reimbursement up to 7.65% of Salary and Housing.

Housing; the Total Effective Salary includes all Housing and Utility Allowances paid to the Minister.

Expense Reimbursements; the Total Effective Salary does not include any reimbursements made to the Minister if they are included in the Accountable Reimbursement Plan of the church. If the Minister submits proper documentation for expenses in the area of Auto/Mileage, Travel, Study Leave, Books and Professional Expenses, and Other allowances, then these reimbursements do not become a part of Wages for W-2 purposes or a part of the Total Effective Salary.

Fringe Benefits: the Total Effective Salary does not include any Fringe Benefits paid on behalf of the Minister for Medical and Pensions Dues, Life Insurance Premiums (up to $50,000 of coverage), Cafeteria Plan payments, etc.

For the Treasurer's benefit the Board of Pensions has a Dues Calculator on their website so you can enter in the appropriate information of the Pastor's call or employee's salary and it will calculate for you the amount of the expected dues. Go to www.pensions.org and look for the tab labeled "calculators."

61-Anticipating Financial Problems

The Treasurer should have a firm grasp of the financial picture of the church and make every effort to notify the Finance Committee and / or Session when he/she sees irregularities. These could include;

*donors who have greatly reduced their pledge to the church,

*pledges or offerings not coming in as strong as expected,

*the need to move money from Reserves,

*unexpected or unplanned for bills,

*areas of the budget that are spending way past expectation.

It is not the role of the Treasurer to worry about or fix these concerns but to notify the proper people to get things appropriately adjusted in time to avert a crisis.

There may be systems the Treasurer can suggest to the Finance Committee or Session that would help the church better "control" income and expenses. These could include quarterly mailings to the congregation to communicate the financial situation, or developing a form for reimbursements which require a supervisorial signature, or other "systems" that will help the church increase income and decrease unwanted spending.

Again, it is not the responsibility of the Treasurer to fix these things, just to communicate the concerns to the powers that be.

62-Session Minutes

Make it a regular practice that the Treasurer receives a copy of all Session minutes so they can determine what financial actions the Session took. This way the Treasurer will be able to anticipate future expenditures or quickly comply with the wishes of the Session.

Often in churches a decision is made in the Session but never communicated to the Treasurer and things fall through the cracks. Having the minutes on a regular basis would help to alleviate some of these issues.

63-Continually Preparing for Annual Review

The Treasurer should always keep in mind annual review that will come at the end of the year. All of the record keeping, documentation, systems, processing, and the like will become a factor in a smooth Review. Anything not properly documented or processed will create extra work for the volunteers when they come to look over the finances of the church and report their findings to the Session. Why not make your job run more efficiently and make the reviewers jobs more pleasant by having well thought out systems in place and continually requiring clear and thorough documentation?

Resources

(Intentionally Blank)

64-Resources

The references in this section are intentionally vague because content in side of websites change from time to time.

- **Articles on church finances and tax law**.
  - Written by Frank Sommerville, non-profit attorney.
- **The Board of Pensions** of the Presbyterian Church (U.S.A.).
  - www.pensions.org you should find resources:
  - *Tax Guide for Ministers*, updated annually.
  - *Understanding Effective Salary*, how effective salary is determined.
  - *Frequent Tax Questions and Answers* for Treasurers, Administrators, etc.
  - *Housing Allowance Letter*.
  - *Dues Calculator* for determining the amount of dues the church will owe based upon the Pastor's terms of call or the employee's salary.
- **The Book of Order,** Part II Constitution of the Presbyterian Church (U.S.A.).
- **The Church Guide to Employment Law**, by Julie L. Bloss, J.D., available on Amazon.com.
- **Church Law and Tax, Richard Hammar, J.D.,**
  - www.churchlawandtax.com.
  - Variety of resources on **all phases of Church Law and Tax Law** and Employment Law.
- **Church Mutual Insurance** – www.churchmutual.com.
- **The Church Treasurer's Manual,** available by contacting the author **edd@breeden.us**.
- **Employee Handbook**, **Presbyterian Church (U.S.A.)** Human Resources Office.

- **Financial Review Guide** – An Annual Financial Review Committee Checklist, ask edd@breeden.us
- **Guidelines for Session Personnel Committees**,
- **GuideOne Insurance** – www.guideone.com.
- **Insurance Board** – www.insuranceboard.org.
  - **Your Church: Employer and Small Business.**
- **The Internal Revenue Service Publications**, www.irs.gov.
  - Employer's Tax Guide, **Circular E.**
  - **Charitable Contributions.**
  - Determining the **Value of Donated Property.**
  - **Social Security** for Members of Clergy and Religious Workers.
  - **Tax Guide for Churches** and Other Religious Organizations.
  - **Taxable and Non-Taxable Income.**
  - **Travel, Entertainment and Gift Expenses.**
- **The Office of Legal / Risk Management** of the General Assembly.
  - **Legal Resource Manual** *for Presbyterian Church (U.S.A.) Middle Governing Bodies and Churches,* (to download a copy go to www.pcusa.org and search for Legal Resource Manual)
  - **Employee or Independent Contractor** – Published by Office of Risk Management PC(USA), A twenty (20) factor checklist to determine if a person should be treated as an employee or independent contractor.
- **The Presbyterian Foundation.**
  - www.presbyterianfoundation.org.
  - **Ministry Toolbox.**
  - **Stewardship Resource Center.**
  - **Stewardship Manual: A Guide to Year-Round Stewardship Planning,**

- **Session Personnel Committee Guidelines**, available for download on the pcusa.org website.
- **Social Security and Other Information** for Members of the Clergy and Religious Workers, Internal Revenue Service Publication 517.
- **Stewardship Kaleidoscope Conference** – Held annually and open to all attenders; put on by a joint team from the PC USA and the Lutheran Church of America.
  - **Plenty of good resources available from past conferences.**
  - www.stewardshipkaleidoscope.org
- **Your Church: Employer and Small Business**. www.InsuranceBoard.org

www.ingramcontent.com/pod-product-compliance
Lightning Source LLC
Chambersburg PA
CBHW072014230526
45468CB00021B/1464